Into Light

Poems by
M. D. Friedman

Liquid Light Press

ISBN: 978-0-9985487-8-4

Liquid Light Press
poetry for the heart
www.liquidlightpress.com

Book & Cover Design by M. D. Friedman
www.MDFriedman.com

Author Photo on Back Cover by Robert Mattson
www.DownStageImages.com

~ for Mariamne

Contents

after being told i look good for 67
(on my 57th birthday)

damn fluorescent lights
damn the buzz
laugh lines shadow deeper
veins ridge up

the window glares
at my reflection
(so much depends
on lighting)

I shiver in the building
see my own breath
the grim reaper sits down next to me
tells me Jewish mother jokes

aging is a paradox
our engines slow as the scenery
speeds by ever faster
everything breaks on this train

the news sounds
like a rag flapping
on a barbwire fence
it takes longer to chew

my bones creak and something new hurts
yet my mind grows more playful
my heart more childlike
eyes brighten on a dimming world

slowly we turn back into light

Acrophobia

in memory of Mike Adams

rain bites
goose-bumped skin
shivers bones

lilac whiffs on languid wind
and that smell
when rain first tames the dust

brings me once again
to who I am
(in this dying cage of skin)

between warm speckled rays
thunder hems & haws
clears its throat of cloud

the old lineman mumbles
can't work
in the lightning

only sporadic strikes
riddle the ambivalent sky
but I had to agree

it was a yellow afternoon
and there is never
a better place to stand

than where your feet
meet the ground
nearby a flash rips through

I wouldn't go up there either
not if I had a say about it
not now

probably never

Girl Braiding Hair

She combs her hair as if to untangle
the tussle of his touch, powders plum skin
still stinging from his grizzled tentacle,
over is over when the pain won't end.

Elderberry lips are smeared red to hide
the ache, and the baby that was to be,
a hated thing, no longer lives inside,
over is over, at last she writhes free.

Emerging from tide pools, how her eyes swell,
gleam blue, brim briny with bright tears of *no*;
her anguish, a warped lens, a fractured shell,
over is over wherever she goes.

Easy enough to layer her young hand
full of hair on the red strand tightly held
hand upon strand upon hand upon strand,
over is over when love's flame is quelled.

Not so simple to grab another fist
full of life, or to be braided again,
when what blooms and wrenches within is missed,
over is over when love's made a sin.

forever trespass

(can be read down or across)

like someone	the sun	this is why I
could own this	cracked creek	am possessed
	it eats my eyes	these hungry words
sure	underneath	the roiling red juice
it changes	the marbled light	pours from my bones
with each step	fish trespass	and I drink
I walk in	the turbid stream	of myself
not so	swollen	my breath becomes light
you would	from my melting	my living
notice		yes
not all	words run	the bright air
at once	the poet	owns this body
this land	wind me up	as it
possesses us	like a toy boat	rides the blood

When I Did Not Have My Camera

The old man in the sculpture park
sleeps on the sun-streamed, bronze bench
weathered arm of flesh in languid embrace
on the sculpted woman's flawless neck.

How long have they been here together like this,
the dreamer and the artifact?

Noteworthy

She wrote a note to herself
to stand on one leg.
This is not unusual.

She always writes notes.
I see her standing
steady as a flamingo.

She does this
to improve
her balance,

practices while cooking
to save time,
topless in the heat of day.

Her cheeks puff out
with a mouthful of water
to hold in tears from slicing onions.

As is her way,
at the bottom of the note,
she draws a heart.

Picasso's Violin
In response to the sculpture by Jodie Bliss

he plays Within
the wind under
the skin of a glass eye
Wiggles the bOw in
the rain belOw
sighs as tears
blow Out
of his mind

Li Po Returns to His Lover in the Night

in honor of the Poet Immortal who drowned
trying to embrace the moon's reflection in a river

It is magical indeed
how I fall without suffering
through the watered moonlight,
how still I breathe
with the breeze.

Can you hear me
rattle the leaves
over your head,
moan (like your new lover)
against the warm earth?

Do you feel me? My vague
hand sweeps the wayward
hair from your glistening eyes
as gently as the pale, languid
lotus petal falls from the blossom

behind your ear, swirls
against the silken robes
crumpled at your feet.
Though tonight you find me in every
wisp of wind, in every sigh, tomorrow,

do not bemoan my moving on.
For with each breath,
I come and go.
Like moon-laden tears of dew,
I vanish in a blaze of light.

Two as One

Through different eyes we see the same,
not the waterfall, but the water falling,
no longer sculpted by gravity,
turning weightless, and in this moment
finding its own shape.

We turn our gaze and see together
how the sinuous rock walls
and the fingers of the trees are fluid too,
how it all shimmers and sways,
a rippled mirage whirling
back into sudden clarity.

We find our own shape,
here on the edge of this liquid cliff,
gushing with the splash and clamor of the falls,
flowing in and out of each other,
like breath, two as one.

Through the Schism

an invisible fissure
splits light from
the flowing colors
that paint our day

it opens like a portal
for those who know it's there
you were there
you saw it with me

how the backlit birds
never broke formation
simply winked from the liquid sky
to somewhere else

The Goddess Ate at Arby's

Hers is a difficult beauty, from a world
where the night is blistered gold, and
dark trees bristle with blue, hair-like leaves.
Feathery fish swim the summer wind,
while eyeless serpents burrow
with flat, black beaks
through silvery whiffs of sand.
What she ate is still a mystery.

Perhaps salad. Perhaps she lives on air.
What matters, though, is all of sudden
there she was as amber and shimmering
as the failing light of a dying candle.
(I still see her, pulsing on the curtain of my eyelids.)
She was chewing something, grudgingly
inhaling the oily smoke of rush hour,
exhaling our choking world like a sputtering tailpipe.

Translucent, dreamlike, iridescent, this creature
of sparkle and moon milk, sat three tables away
as real as the flickering fluorescent lights,
chomping down her lunch. Disregarding all signage,
she wore
no shoes, or skin, for that matter.
What clothes she had licked her like flame.
Leaving a trail of diamond dust, she slid resplendent
into the yellow plastic booth where I sat, as if to chat,

yet the goddess did not speak.
Nor did I, although I could feel
the pain in her soul. Sad as a black hole,
veins surging blue starlight,
bleeding as calmly as a fading red giant,
her lungs wheezed laboriously with each expansion
and contraction of the universe. I wanted desperately
to help her, to somehow make things right,

but drunk with greed, we frenzy feed
upon the glowing bowl of her heart,
lapping up her luminous essence
like a pack of gluttonous dogs. There is no
end to what we take, while her breath
whispers through all that lives
she is dying.

Lesson of the Garden

It is not my breath rustling the leaves.
I sit monochrome in the speckled light,
still as shade, almost awake. This morning,
everything has changed. Gleam on green,

last night's rain loads the labyrinth of leaves.
I watch clematis blue
stretch celestial.
Whether dusty sage or prickly pear sweet,

it's not my intention to change a thing,
to favor towering foxglove over
purslane's yellow bud or twisted clover.

A fleecy head of dandelion
harms not the noble, indigo iris.
Now that summer is finally upon us,

there is no need to name a thing a weed.
I hear the distant drone of mowers.
My neighbors scurry, scrape and pound.
The bursting burr, the cinnamon tendrils

of climbing rose, the pink-tipped petals
of bindweed blossoms, the healing echinacea,
all vibrate with sunlight, all have their niche, their time
to flourish.
Where in this vibrant land is my place to thrive?

The answer surrounds me.
All that matters is to be truly wild,
to vine my heart around the roots of love:

unfurl the luminous lotus within.
Listen how the grass flattened by my feet
springs back to life as I walk away.

Crossing Rabbit Ears Pass
June 22, 2005

The moon rubs against the earth
and they all come out,
wild-eyed from the forest,
pale shades from milk-lit meadows,
out to the edge of our passing.
From atop a precarious ledge above the dreaming
    land,

from between the snowy lips of the mouth of mist,
from upon a whispering bed of crumpled grass,
they smell our heat
rising like thick vapors from a scalding spring.
They know all life is woven together
by pulsing threads of breath.

They come this full moon night,
this solstice, to see us.
First, rabbit frozen in headlights,
still as ice. Next,
hungry fox glancing back at us
on his way to chase rabbit.

One deer, then a dozen others,
moving as one,
in and out of shadow trees,
prancing across the swollen earth,
like dry leaves swept along
by creamy moon breath.

Puma,
lit from behind,
emerges ethereal
out of the shadows,
graceful, tranquil, emanating
the presence of raw power,

eyes burning like small golden suns.
Each hair on her body electric,
she hovers glistening, trailing her corporal frame,
a ghost cat, rippling like a reflection,
almost disappearing, as she shakes the silver
from her moonlit coat.

There was no sound, yet somehow,
she vibrates, flesh alive with breath,
she mews the mystic melody of our meanderings
through the dapple forest, over liquid cliffs,
into this most magical place,
this sacred meadow of light.

She knows of
our return to each other
after half a life apart,
and without words,
she blesses our joining
and is gone.

i wish now

i wish now
i was with you
under this moon
as full as my anticipation

i want now to be
skin to skin within
your arms again
emptied of my desperation

as if our lives
between had
never happened
freed of regret

would that i could
have known then
what now i know
and we again first met

alone in this darkness
i begin to pretend
the same moon
rides your night

strong and fragile
as the eggshell
moonlight
i reach for you tonight

She Has a Mortgage on My Body and a Lien on My Soul

inspired by a blues song by Robert Johnson

Driving too far too fast to see her again.
No one else will do.
She touches me with subtle delight,
like how the lake scatters
the sunlight raining down
after a storm.

I am taken by how much I need this.
I have come so far to get here again
with this woman I have wanted since
that Poco concert, when she surprised me
from behind and circled me within her arms
beneath the stars spinning like whirling diamonds.

It comes back to this,
more than thirty years later,
this rebellion against caring,
this reaching for closeness and then running
from the love I need,
this fear of having what I've always wanted.

I am addicted.
I will steal from whatever
life I've made for myself
for yet another fix of her.
I need her more,
the more we are together.

Sweat beads up upon my sweat.
I tremble at the painful thought
of losing her again.
I will never let her go.
She has a mortgage on my body,
a lien on my soul.

Spring Love Poem

Not only the thirsty seeks the water
but the water seeks the thirsty as well.
  ~ Rumi

I reach with my heart
into the pool of you,
the ripples of our yearning
splinter our reflection.

Here in the lotus of breath,
whirl the stars and moon
in sensual dance.
Immersed in fragrant emersion,

we are closer than touch.
The air you breathe,
I breathe,
closer than the blood that fills our hearts.

I have known this forever.
I remember each time
I am with you,
I have known forever

that somehow we will
always be together.
I have lived for this
when nothing else made sense.

Know Where to Go Crazy

He is going nowhere, deliberately.
~ Elizabeth Robinson

I've been here before,
where the rain cuts through like shards of glass
drives me deep into the mouth of fog,

frozen, frosted with lacy flakes.
This is nowhere to go crazy.
When I move again, I return to somewhere,

anywhere there is something.
I'm done with that circle of tears
where dark fears fall from a lightning cracked sky.

It's over. The only way out is in.
There is nothing to say. It's time to leave.
There's nowhere to go, so I'm off.

It might as well be a picnic,
with this frayed tablecloth
I keep in my back pocket to blow my nose.

There is nothing to take. A bleeding
wafer of heart between two loaves
of breath is all I need.

I linger in the ghosted meadow.
My soul in its blue bottle
stirs the rocks to breathe.

I want only to blaze my own way,
to climb my high green hill
where each star shines alone.

Sure, I'll miss the warmth of the crowd,
the clap of strangers bumping into me, but
the broken music takes me now, ears stuffed into
    brain.

No time to stay. No reason for more of the sane.
My screams fall like paper. I leave what is left
for another to write.

No desire for the ashes of this burning world.
My breath fogs my glasses.
In a dark way, I am filled with light.

I am ready. I've had no sleep for weeks.
My eyes open from looking inward.
I have sharpened my teeth.

Inside, it never changes. Every way I turn
leads back. I awake ever closer to sleep.
The edge of my dream cracks with beauty.

I wish I could take you. Here in the middle
of nowhere, there is so much to share.
The silence shatters into light.

It is a miracle just to be alive.

Everything in Beauty

Iridescent beetles scurry over soft black loam,
rose sheds wrinkled pink, petal by petal,
crystal tears flood eyes laughing bright,
stealthy hawk thumps grazing rabbit,
grumbling thunder ricochets
down the canyon, yellow finch flaps
black blur of wings, amber sap
glows on red mushroom caps, the lonely
whine of distant traffic on a wet road,
rain-dark log seems to breathe,
rippled mud at clear water's edge
glitters with pyrite, bumping bodies
board night bus, magenta bleeds to black,
spider web twinkles with the last light.

How supremely important to celebrate
each flash as it fades,
drink in what shimmers,
embrace the joy that lingers,
take in more than we name.

The Old Barn

lodged between
shadow and splinter
the red paint molts
grays, crinkles
vermilion leaves
molder into black earth
pulse with broken light

i, too
leave myself
graceful in decay
find myself
abandoned
my body
rippled with light

one short season ago
this field erupted
buzzed vibrant red
whirred with hummingbirds,
a crush of bees burst
into molten magenta
into bloom after vivid bloom

now weathered barnwood
wormed with scarlet sunset
suffers the gleaming urgency
of fading light,
the old barn and I hoard our
pneuma
swallow hard
against a rush of wind

Memory Care

for Anita

I heard some of you got your families
living in cages, tall and cold,
and some just stay there and dust away
past the age of old.
    ~ Jimi Hendrix "Up From the Skies" (1968)

age breaks the cage
the canary
lingers

the soft-boiled egg
of her mind cracks
open

day after
yellowed day
nothing stays

each morning
she rises to a
fresh world

plays out childhood
from vague finish
to start

rides the glass
slide down foggy
mirrors

she smiles
as she waits
for the flash

Selling Ourselves

Parenthood is always a gamble,
a crap shoot fusion of egg and sperm,
the flesh explosion of another life into ours,
an invitation to the ultimate challenge of being human
and the associated fallout from striving

to be an ever-better parent.
We seem to forget ourselves
under the mushroom cloud of the nuclear family,
putting aside our wants for someone else.
Every child comes with a price:

things we settle for, dreams
we let go of, promises we make to ourselves
but never keep.
Then these children become their own people,
grow from parasitism to mutualism.

We are always seeking
a better life for those we spawn,
perhaps this ticket is a winner,
or perhaps another whiner.
Maybe one day they will

even buy our story.
This morning we wake like every morning,
make our tired bed, fix our low-fat breakfast,
and we sell ourselves again. We wonder at where
the time has gone.

Then one morning
all children wake up,
make their own bed, fix their own breakfast,
go out into the world
and sell themselves.

We wonder when they grew up and how they know
to speak, to walk, to even breathe
without our guidance, but what we hope the most is
they learn before it's too late –
no price is enough to ask for your life.

Coupled Socks

It is not the coupled socks that interest me
as I fold clean laundry on the unmade bed,
but those newly found ones that arrive each week
without a partner. I have always taken it as proof

of the porous nature of the universe, a weekly lecture
on the impermanence of relationship, a poignant
    reminder
of personal taboo and of how my own conventional
    nature
frowns on making my own pairs.

A black with a brown, or perhaps, a sporty
red-striped one with solid white would be a start.
After a few washes it is hard to tell
blue from black anyway.

Still, as regularly as the evening news,
unmatched "pairs" show up
on these love strewn sheets
where, just hours ago, we coupled.

I wonder why I continue
to mate only matched pairs,
even after that one wild night when I defiantly
wore a black with a blue, and nothing bad happened.

Parting Shots

It's not working.
You're too old.
You're too immature.
You're not my type.

I'm not ready for this.
You're too intense.
Nothing matters to you.
You never take anything seriously.

You take, take, take.
I miss what we had.
You try too hard.
We never tried at all.

I need some space.
You're smothering me.
You are always gone.
You take me for granted.

It's not you. It's me.
You deserve someone better.
You deserve something more.
You deserve to rot in hell.

We have nothing in common.
You remind me of my ex.
All you care about is yourself.
You're a selfish bastard.

We've been pretending.
You never listen.
You hate my friends.
I hope we can always be friends.

My Will

I'll make a broken music, or I'll die.
~ Theodore Roethke

The music is already broken.
I stand tangled
in flames and briers,
my body aching
against the warped
metallic sky.
The wind comes
like jagged pieces of glass
and fills my ears.

I fear the music of the wind.
I fear the black edges
of its lightning.
I know the crystal thunder
that follows.
It comes as noiselessly
as a fistful of daggers
flashing to its mark,
shatters my heart.

All around me blink
the green/white eyes of aspens,
blink the fire/ice eyes that see in all directions.
I, too, try to dance with the motionless sun.
I cry the song that tears into throat,
slap hot rocks with feet.
It is no use. I am crushed like a fly
against the glass that keeps me from the world.
This is nowhere to die.

I stand against the wind
suffocated by the air rushing in.
Like a small child, I close my eyes to disappear.
I am blind. I am hiding.
I am the fire that lives in the ashes.
There is no light,
only this groaning heat.
This is not death.
Why am I still pretending?

I prop my eyes open
with white slivers of hawk bone,
lie on my back
in the haunted dust,
and stare into the sun,
and stare
as the sky boils off,
until all that surrounds me
disappears.

As the cracked marbles of my eyes go out,
I gnaw the searing white flesh of sun,
suck the open salt from its blood,
until there is no music,
until the whirlwind of color and life
falls through the black hole of my mind.
We cannot escape this loneliness, even in
death.
I leave my song to the silence,
my soul to the wind.

Upon Turning Fifty

An aged man is but a paltry thing,
A tattered coat upon a stick, unless
Soul clap its hands and sing, and louder sing
For every tatter in its mortal dress,
  ~ W. B Yeats from "Sailing to Byzantium"

When young, I bragged
I must be 2000 years old;
what passed for new
seemed weirdly familiar.

When young, I knew too many
who suicide and murder wasted.
Now friends younger than I suffer
cancer, heart attacks and strokes.

I feel my age everyday.
There is nothing to brag about,
nor would I trade wisdom's
cool water for my salty youth.

I feel lucky to feel old.
While performing last week,
a 200-volt surge
glued my hand to a microphone.

My fist tightened around
the screaming wand of death.
I had no control,
no way to let go.

The jolt flopped
me onto my back.
I jerked and flapped,
fishlike on the cement floor.

Electrified excruciation, jaws clinched down
on a spluttering spark,
muted cries wrenched my throat,
I writhed fetal on cold concrete.

A young stranger risked his life, kicked
the searing, needle-stabbing mic
from my charred, disobedient hand.
I lay sputtering, a stuttering ball of amnesia.

Electrocution leaves you humble,
clinging to life with open hands.
I drop my hurt-filled past
like papery ash upon the spring grass.

I live afresh in ragged poems,
rip revision after revision,
stitch odd nuance and false rhyme
to patch a magic sail.

My soul
of colored crystal,
rocks like a ship
upon an endless sea of light.

I relish the honeymoon
groans of wooden masts,
attend to my sail as it fills
and flaps like a heart.

Borne so fortunately forward,
I am gratefully
energized
by each new breath.

It's Easy to Be Normal
for Brent

I can pass for normal if I really try. I put on deodorant, and
    it seems to help.
Just yesterday, someone asked me for the time, and I
    said, "1:36,"
even though I always carry a sprig of the herb in my
    pocket
in case that question comes up. It's easy to be normal.

A husky voiced phone survey woman asked, "Sex?"
I told her, "Male." Just like that. At the grocery store,
    though,
I lost it. The bagger inadvertently brushed my hand and
    said,
"Paper or plastic?" I said, "It's skin. Isn't that normal?"

Most of the time, if I concentrate,
I can ignore all those variant
meanings that come to mind,
and figure out what others want from me.

Isn't that what normal is,
doing what others expect instead of being who I am?
The most important thing is to try to be like everybody
    else.
My biggest problem, perhaps, is I don't watch television.

In polite conversation, I have found it helps
to nod often, even if nothing makes sense.
I probably shouldn't even talk
about peppers. When the waiter asks,

"Ground pepper?" I say, "Yes, please." Simple enough.
The problem comes when he says, "Just say when."
I usually say nothing. When he gets tired, he walks away.
What I want to say is, "Whenever the grinder is empty."

Lately, I have started to carry
my own bottle of pepper sauce
for places where ketchup is the only
condiment. It makes things easier.

I wonder if anybody really is normal,
if everybody is nodding because nothing makes sense.
I think I could fit in if we all stopped pretending,
but then people take too much too seriously.

I could be normal, if it paid enough, but it's truly
    overrated.
It's certainly no way to raise children. I guess I should
    spend more time
worrying about how things look. Also, it would help,
to occasionally be on time, but then there is always

that poem I am working on that won't let me go.
Somehow, I get by. I have a good life, I must say.
There is really no reason to change,
unless, of course, I spill hot sauce on my shirt.

The Super Bowl of the Muse
for Amanda Gorman

Let's turn it on.
I mean really turn it on.
Let's turn on it.
It's time to turn it around.
Let's watch it
from the inside.

Let's turn it over before it's over.
This time we'll turn that flashing
fat screen upside down.
We'll strip the cold fire from its flicker
and tickle its underbelly as it
jiggles topless in an electric dance.

Let's over tip the dust bunnies,
those cheerleaders of neglect,
as they shake their chalky booties
bristling with blue light.
Let's stuff their sequined G-strings
green with sweaty money.

Let's transform it all
until it turns us on.
It's the New American Dream.
It's never over until the fat lady sings,
and this time we'll listen to her words.
It's her song that matters now.

It is the Super Bowl of the Muse.
The Big Game in the Big Easy.
And this year it's even bigger, better, bolder.
It's more colorful, more eclectic,
more engaging
and less real than ever.

Can you imagine?
Even the commercials have something new to say:
a middle-aged Allen Ginsberg doing the shimmy.
His hairy belly bulges out from under
his red, white and blue
flag tank top.

Crowned in a rainbow of fireworks,
Allen gulps down a chilled diet Pepsi,
like secret, sparkling nectar from Shangri-La,
as if the red, white and blue can
was filled with the lusty dreams of his youth.
Our Allen simply belches, "om," twinkling his timeless
    grin.

It's all happening now.
It's Super Overtime.
We're into Sudden Death.
Let's rock with the rockers.
Let's roll it over in the fake green grass
of our imagination.

Let's rewind the rerun, fast forward it to the end.
Play it backwards to start all over again.
This is our new beginning.
Let's put a giant magnifying glass
over the top of the Superdome
and set it ablaze.

Let's tear down the old goals.
Just imagine 100,000 people
all paying big bucks to sit with the big cheese
in this quaking maze of stands and fans,
all snapping their fingers frantically
and pounding their feet for more poetry!

Millions more having Super Slam Parties.
Think of it –
poets going to Disneyland!
Everybody everywhere stops everything
for a single afternoon.
Even people who don't like poetry feign passion,

munch down word chips
dipped in dark image,
take off on hot wings,
sport inky berets
to impress
their own fickle muse.

We're so entranced by how
the fresh blood still sputters
from the cheap shot
in s l o w m o t i o n over and over,
we forget our own surging turmoil.
Again, we angrily boo the fumbled phrase.

Yes – all of America out of control
cheering wildly for more
graceful word play.
The yellow flags of syntax
thrown down without penalty,
we can almost taste sweet victory.

What's a split infinitive or even a sentence fragment
when the Great Win is in sight! Oh yes, just think of it!
Everybody everywhere screaming at once,
slurring their meaningless slogans into a single soulful
    chant,
throwing their hands to the sky
in an endless human wave.

Our real heroes are on the field,
taking their licks for the team.
Slamming themselves into each other
like bugs flattened on a windshield.
We who sit and watch from above
spring to our feet in one overwhelming motion!

Cross-eyed from the hard hits,
shaking with exhaustion,
dripping Gatorade,
smeared with mud and blood,
the players frantically
guard the gridiron,

falling finally forward
into one great groping
sweaty flesh hill,
melting down like a pile
of ice cubes
abandoned and draining.

Counting down the final seconds, we stumble,
stagger and stomp almost in unison,
drunk on our own inner revelation.
Pregnant with joy, swollen with pride, we flail about
beer-bloated and convulsing in syncopated steps,
sinfully drenched in the sweet sweat of our synergy.

In a single moment of satori,
it is too clear
that despite all the hype,
the money and noise,
there has never been anyone
on the field.

The final buzzer
screeches as poignantly
as a virgin bride
learning her husband
is not the gentle man
she thought she married.

Who will play
the Winner
now the harsh
light of truth
has finally turned
upon us?

The King of the United States

"I am the King of the United States,
and we can fix this mess,"
Dad proclaims from his nursing home throne.
"It is good to walk," I reply.

We carefully negotiate the splintered rafters
shattered by Parkinson's, the ink blots of mold
where the dark water seeps in.
Pieces of his life bob idly in brackish pools.

Fear and anger swell within him,
black springs riddled with reflections,
rippling with frustrations he forgets as quickly as they
    arrive.
We pick our way across a broken web of memories

dribbling with brine and shuffle to the outside. He
    knows
I stopped at the store. He enjoys the grapes and
    chocolate,
whistles in reply to the afternoon birdsong
and offers to make me the Minister of Trade.

Feasting in America

I don't remember what I ate that day.
The deli floor was bowed as if
the indecisive shifting of shoes
had settled it into a tired smile
smoothed by feet
and friction.

I don't remember what I ate.
Perhaps lasagna,
I do remember pepperoncinis
on a wonderful salad.
We were moving Dad
from a temporary nursing home

in North Miami
to a nicer place
closer to Mom.
His raving racist roommate,
stung the Black orderly
with a bitterness exclusive

to the beaten and senile.
Dad, silent and staring,
intently chewing his lower lip,
had not been attended to
when we arrived
that muggy Sunday afternoon.

Many of his clothes were
missing, like his front teeth,
knocked out when they revived him
from the near drowning.
I think he knew me
as his son.

He walked with the slow shuffle
of Parkinson's decay, his back
round as a snail's shell,
bent as if leaning over
an imaginary cane.
It was an authentic Italian deli

worn but not changed
through the years, holding on
as the neighborhood morphed
from Italian to Jewish to Black to Cuban to Haitian,
always heavy with the smell of garlic,
an olfactory landmark in a world of ethnic flux.

Our talk was of fresh, steaming bread,
and how Dad always said
you can tell a good restaurant by the salad.
I remember walking along fogged glass cases
filled with waves of lasagna and piles of hot sausage,
sturdy blue bowls of pasta, white and red sauces,

but all I remember eating was salad.

The Last Time Dad Opened His Eyes

His eyes, the color of fog,
blind as night,
reaching out of the driftwood of his body
in place of the arms he could not move,

held me in a way no arms could.
He, who had given me everything,
now gave me this final gift,
our last time together.

This lover of sunsets and old trees,
his face now a shadow, cast down by disease,
lay rough and limp as parchment,
an old map washed ashore by time.

In every dark wrinkle,
through each drawn crease,
over the strangely smooth hollows of his cheeks,
flowed the gentle kindness that marked his life.

As this, his last sunset,
broke in exquisite sadness,
there were no colored clouds
to usher in the pending dusk.

All his strength went into his breathing,
all his will, to open his eyes
the color of fog,
heavy with the last light.

A Pair of Apple Poems

1.
One apple was left in the poetry workshop snack basket. It was frosted with wax. Pale yellow flakes buckled its skin the way aspen leaves freckled the dry grass. The apple leaned to one side as if to better hear the silent musings, the scraping of the poets' pens, as if a fruit could be plumped up by raw ink or could mysteriously feed on the magic of words and fidgeting dreams. Maybe the apple wanted to write a life of its own and fall far from the tree of its beginning.

The noise of the poets was strangely reassuring to the apple. Shrewdly musical, their rhythms reminded the apple of when, in its youth, it had danced with abandon, profoundly shaken by the click of branches fencing with the wind. Although those biting storms in the nights of its forming terrified the apple to its core, the grating sounds of the poets now flooded the apple with a cinnamony sense of warmth and comfort. This apple, picked to sell before it could find the ground on its own, now lay cool and quiet in my hand.

Packed with the hidden power of sunlight, its sweetness a little too green, firmly and fully imperfect, this pome draws me out of my longing. I can tell by how its seeds like worms find my mind dark and fertile as an old horse pasture, this apple still thinks it is falling. After enduring the rough passage of its short life and the assiduous gnawing of my mouth, it falls into my blood.

2.

An apple fell on Einstein's head. It puzzled him. Gravity
had already been discovered. Matter and energy had
been seen only yesterday leaving the cheap motel
together. So what of this knock on his melon? Was God
just checking if his mind was ripe? Was it the routine
ringing of a cosmic alarm clock reminding him to be
awake? Were the Fibonacci stars that crosscut the
apple's seeds plotting to plant their pervasive patterns
in the gray furrows of his grateful brain?

Although I am sure he grasped the full gravity of the
event, Albert shyly released a half smile as if he were
mildly entertained. It was the reluctant, yet
irrepressible, grin of a man amused and relieved at the
same time. "Somethings go better unnoticed," he was
heard to say. This was disappointing for the apple, who
had received only the smallest bylines for the force
equally exerted on Newton's noggin. Yet, Einstein
knew the fingerprint of interconnection when it
pressed down on him. If nothing else made sense, it
seems apples are always falling.

Albert took it as a compliment. He kept the apple,
pared it for lunch, and so laid bare its core,
prematurely exposing the tender vessels of the next
generation and its seeping nectar to the persistent
browning of his breath.

Highway 93 as KFML Goes Off the Air, 1975

no new neon
fooly cool jewels
this way
but snow blows
and she-frog
sings lung-tongued
through the wizard's gizzard.

she dog.
me dogged cat.
I hear fear air.
click off. no more frantic static.
no more satanic
her hum.
only ME sing song through sway way.

she's black cat back now
with high beams steaming.
she's yo yo mean screams
with blind eyes blinding!
ME SCREAM!!
lights fight
brights on/off
ice highway.

twinkle twinkle

quiet sky.

I Miss You

It is the month of ravens, the time
of liquid light. It has been a long year
within the golden eye of the imagination.
There was much to see,
yet nothing endures,
and I cannot bear to be without you
for another day. My feet
freeze in place. There is no getting away
from what may break. Even my shadow is
brittle, cracks like ice beneath the vacuous sun.
In the great spruce behind our home,
three ravens squeak out caws like twisted nails
from frigid bark, change positions as they ladder up,
branch by branch, but the small one, a female
I think, is first to the top. Yesterday,
after the snow came, the solar disk
whimpered behind a wispy smudge of cloud,
shimmered dreamy and moonlike, and a lone eagle
shuttled its way across the steel wool sky.
It is the month of luminous mist,
of the burning bite of hoarfrost,
when the cold takes possession
of its own, and the charred
raven brings the glowing gift
to those whose words freeze in the mouth.
As slanted rays of shrouded light
fall from the ash,

I am left to ask,
"What brings you to me in the night?
Will the knit of need and knot of time
hold only when legs are woven tight?"
My fabric frays without you.
Here in the chill of the crystalline dawn,
the gray and glittered grit of the perpetual thaw,
I climb the murky tree of my mind, ascending
limb by limb into the stark sky of heart. Each day away,
I ache within the hollow of my bones;
like the morning star, I bleed into the bluster of day.

The Third Moon Full in a Season of Four

The gathering storm eats
the true-blue moon,
a dry wafer, soft, hazy and red
against the tin horizon.

It slips like a shining quarter
into a jukebox of cloud,
lingers gleaming in the dark coin slot
while the sad song plays.

We walk, bundled,
stiff as scarecrows, into
the blustery November dusk.
We came to watch the moonrise,

but what seems striking
is how this diaphanous disk
of sanguine falls pale
and quiet as milkweed fluff

off the edge of the wind
and then is gone. There is
something wonderful in the way
it disappears top first

into ambiguous lips of gray,
like the way you pull me
into your love from whatever
sorry spin my mind puts me in.
We tread our rambling trail
calling owl and raven,
dizzy from the hordes
of squawking geese

hurtling above our heads.
We wonder if the glowing eyes
of coyote will follow us into the dark.
The leaves crisp from the sun

crackle under our feet.
We have become deeply familiar
with how the rippled lake
smooths itself into evening,

how the shadowed land stretches and
yawns as the sleep of winter nears.
We have been this way hundreds of times,
through blistering summer heat and sudden

spring rains. Nothing ever remains,
yet there is something amazing,
something intimate and enduring,
in how our footprints freeze in mud.

This inadvertent capture
of our meandering, frosted
in the last blood of sunset,
glistens as night closes in.

The First Snow

Ice claws the knit cap
pulled snug over ears, and hairs
spring through loops and frizzle,
wild as weeds cracking concrete:
the mind empties like a dandelion
in a yawn of wind.

Ice spit sputters
its bitter electricity,
shatters the night
in a tinfoil scream.
White flakes off,
whirls into myriad colors.

Under the black-blue
bruise of sky,
eye seeds bleed silver.
Those that do not shiver,
freeze and glitter as they fall
into cool crystal.

Through cold moans I drift
dazzled and numb.
I lay my head swirling
on a gleaming
breast of ice
and dream I am warm.

Fetish for the Dark

living
in absolute
vacuum
we space-age poets
marinate our words
dark with gasoline
spark the scarlet
raging stars

collapsing
under the gravity
of light
swallowed by flames
only glittering bones
stand as the last
shattered embers
fall

> *wish upon the ash my love*
> *bathe your breasts in soot*

hollow molten
glass cats
through brittle black
still glow
four feet
over shadows
walk
further into night

As the Stars Go Out

I empty myself,
float darkly
over what the wind has left
from other places
and the things
I leave behind.

I know
my motion
by the way
everything
slips
away.

Like a star that collapses
into itself,
I live alone,
a flower of flame
thriving off the night.

Hard to Breathe

I renounce the violence,
the greed that simmers
through our humanity,

the lies that gouge into my heart.
I ache for the clear ripples of voice,
climbing like clematis the lattice of song.

I plead for a return
to the unifying light
of the forever sun.

We are nearly extinct
in this tar pit
of our making.

We have come to the edge
of suffocating madness.
It is hard to breathe.

The Poets' Way

We mingle memory with skin,
syrupy as sunlight in the late afternoon.
We blend in our tears and dreams,
with a few gizmos
from the wizard's hat,

and cast our motley webs
of light upon the night,
now strewn across sidewalks
like the glitter of windows
broken with pain.

We cannot get in there from here
without going in there again. We dream in
a glass house of our making. It seems as if
it's made of mirrors. There are no
doors, no windows, no reasonable way in.

The inside is bigger than outside.
Inside, everywhere
is a door, a window,
a heart yearning,
a heart humming with love.

Simple Silence

I have walked a thousand poems to get here.
Through dark fields pulsing with the long light,
where the late Yeats whispers
through a dying Roethke,
I have fallen into a land of simple silence.

I have walked a thousand poems to get here.
I need to scream,
but the further I open my mouth,
the less comes out, the louder
the hollow pounding of my heart.

I have walked a thousand poems to get here.
The serif still rests
quietly on the page,
hums like a high-power line
on a windless day.

I have walked a thousand poems to get here.
Words sing serene as sirens,
their eyes living pools
of swirling silence
taking it all in.

I have walked a thousand poems to get here.
Falling in a dream, we fall forever.
(When the waking noise hits, a certain
weightlessness endures.) The unspoken ties
us together in unseen ways.

I have walked a thousand poems to get here.

The Door

The door in my mind
does not open.
It is liquid.
To look at it is to be
swallowed by a mirror.

I walk through.
I am drenched in silver,
seen by night as only a shimmer,
seen by day as stained glass:
my shadow dizzy with colors,
as full of life as warm pond water.

I live a life as normal
as any poet.
No one notices any difference.
Maybe all poets
go through this.

When I die,
the door will splatter.
A wind as dry as fire,
as cold as space,
will bear me away.

Those behind the door
(who speak as one)
will offer me a job.
I will become famous.
I will finally be able
to live off my poetry.

The Lost River

shiny shiny
go now
hungry
thirsty
swallowing
being swallowed
this is it
go now
into the deep
into the dark hole
into thundering quiet
dream now
sleep into the foil
seep onto the coals
sizzling silver
glowing fish
swim within the fire
swim through dull ash
the taste of smoke
leap into the brilliant fall
over rounded rock
over frothing rivulets
into the shining pools
into the shining pool
salty with spawn and sunlight
steaming with life
drink deeply your own blood
eat your fill
go now fisherman
caught in flesh
go now fish
go

Hooked

It is not because no one is home
that this thunder leaves me uneasy.
Rain chants its mantra of falling
no matter what comes to mind.
The rain dashes by like a cat, and the thunder
growls like a dog pulling on its chain.
Water moves, always wearing down,
dissolving whatever is in its way.
Me, I stay put. I could be a tree
how casually I wait for the storm to pass.
The thunder stutters now as if to say,
"Enough already." A muffled squall
rages inside me. It rains here all the time.
The wind pushes the tears back into my eyes.
I open and close the dark window,
open the window because I need to breathe.
I groan in a dialect of thunder no one understands.
Like a drunk stumbling home, I bellow and bawl
until there is nothing to say, until I black out.
I am as hooked and mangled as Hemingway's marlin.
This is what it is like to be old, to be afraid to climb.
(At the top of the tower, the ever turning light
makes a shadow out of everything in its way.)
Once the water, heavy from its journey,
comes to rest, it returns to the purity of the sky.
This is the teaching of the rain, the meaning of our
    breath,
take in deeply what you may but remember always to
    let go.

The Unwinding

Flying is unsettling at first.
There is a certain uncertainty.
Nothing under the feet makes us
uneasy as we climb: we rise as we let go.

An enduring weightlessness,
a nervous tension from within,
holds the droplets together when
the dark water tumbles over the edge of light.

Surreptitiously sliding through
layers of doubt and detail,
we take deliberate care
in falling, whether it be up or down.

We accept the ever shifting
balance between hope and fear.
Our journey is a planned forgetting,
a ritual creating form from fantasy.

As we divorce
ourselves
from our separateness,
we become whole.

Unwinding
is easy as
falling back
into the beauty
of who we are.

March 21, 1994

By the whooshing river
fingerprinted by wind,
by a frothy vortex of equinox,

I sun in my birthday suit
on the white, sinuous throne
of a water-worn log.

Fingernails of wind
rake the river's sparkling skin.
Slowly sliding, darkly clear,

like the river,
I awaken
in the sun.

Between crusted snow
and sun-dried rocks,
is there a force

melding it together?
Or is the liquid sun
smoky water

rounded rock
and touch of wind
welded by whim?

Flowing water is my mantra.
Liquid light fills the space,
billows from within.

The Great Clock

The few trees left
bear fruit of flame that smudge their muddy bark.
There is wisdom in the glowing pomegranates
that whirl hissing to the ground like molten tears.
There is peace in the breathing
blue leaves of sky, a stormy beauty
in the dirty tricks of cloud.

When autumn goes, there is nothing left.
Lonely ashen spikes
fall into simple nonexistence,
await the quenching hush
of winter's white.

The people in the town
peep out through their shutters.
They wait breathless, rolling their big eyes
like bright apples along the slits of shade.
Outside, a single mottled arm directs the traffic of the
    wind,
guides the confused, gritty air
like a conductor shaping Shostakovich.

There is a long, smooth bridge with no one on it.
It opens into the dream, into the shadowed hills
beyond the river of birdsong — a hand of black glass
that reaches into the place we know is there
but can never see when we look for it.

So suddenly spring, the sun
on the bright horizon is falling in on itself,
leaving a magenta dimpled swirl
in the red brick dawn,
like a shimmering pink dust devil
trailing a dazzling wake of metallic feathers,
as if a wild, magic peacock molted as it climbed the sky.

The people flood out,
swelling the streets with human whirlpools,
swinging each other around in ever changing pairs,
an endless chain of arms locking and unlocking,
carelessly flinging each other into another.

A song, more a murmur,
rises from the crowd like smoke.
The rhythm, a hollow pulse,
throbs from the tower of the broken church
in the dead center of the square.
The great clock still tick ticks there,
incessantly monotonous as the beating of their hearts.

The old church burns like a witch, but no one seems to
     care.
New people come into town from across the bridge,
spiraling out of the darkness with no bodies at first.
No one anywhere has a face anyway, only red flame
heads smiling or snarling or opening like hungry mouths.

The clock tower, a black skeleton,
a charcoal sketch of itself,
collapses with a heaving sigh,
a litany of ash, a chiming of embers.
One at a time the people go home,
back to their shuttered houses,
back to their own dark beginnings.

Rerun

I watch myself,
someone must,
an endless rerun
of a canceled sitcom.
There is nothing better on.
With each episode the laugh track builds,
until snickers echo guffaw.
I long for the theme music,
the predictable end, a chance to begin
all over again. I have seen it
all before. I want a commercial
to tell me what I need to be happy.

Everything I say is misunderstood,
as if I am talking in "Igpay Atinlay."
If someone bothers to reply to me,
it sounds like white noise, radio static,
the high buzz of a test pattern,
punctuated by screeching
brakes, the breaking of glass.
On my birthday, I go off
by myself, howl through
the empty night until
there is nothing left of me
but a mournful wail.

Yesterday was not like this,
it was quiet
and made of Silly Putty.
Your face, pressed
warmly against mine,
picked up the colors
of my cartoon.
The sun was a lemony lollipop.
Cars jostled joyfully along
like bright balloons,
bouncing refugees
from the happy party.

The Return of Light

The beasts of light
return to my window,
one by one they swirl down
from the hunched night
falling out of stars
like solstice spangle.

They lock their bright feet
on charred branches
still glowing from their touch.
No, I am not dying. These are not angels.
Like a great Lazy Susan, this world
and the other have not changed places.

A wild, flaming
flock of fluttering,
these creatures of light
gather and settle.
Each understands its place
in the night and how to hold on.

All at once they burst open
with a single luminous chorus of color.
They throw their brilliance
to the clouds, flood
the shadowed false dawn
with throbbing cadmium and crimson.

It is as if my heart, too, exploded,
no longer able to contain my blood
suddenly transfigured
into pulsing scarlet light.
No, I am not dead. The buzz
of my breath still drones within me.

I love the long quiet
of this moment
before they erupt again,
flare with a final burst
of iridescent grandeur
into the flickering, blood-lit sky.

We Fly

We fly this night as if it were
our falling keeping us afloat,
splitting open with light as we go,
bleeding luminance, as if it were our sheen

that draws us up. Our bodies, slight as shadow,
slide freely as the greased
ghost of cloud. Like children chasing the surf,
we frolic in the curling steam

rising from the towering dark smokestacks.
The blackened buildings below
do not pay us any mind; no cold stares note
our play above the city of still.

We slice the air exuberant,
learning the whims of wind as we go,
each clinging to our own
secret pocket of weightlessness.

There is nothing to this
falling out from ourselves. There is nothing
more real. Like the graceful craning heron,
we arrive to where we reach.

The Long Drive Home from a Gig at 3 AM

The pavement is not real.
The stars, like salt
spilled on black velvet,
show no sign of life,
stare like glass eyes from space.

Sugar Blue whines
and growls his hollow ache,
moans his hot harmonica wind
through brass and plastic,
charges the vacant night with longing.

Everyone who
ever plays, stretches
for that note
missing from the chord
that binds us.

Sugar digs it out, slams it
down on the rough road
like black ice, scrapes
it against raw face
like sandpaper.

Inside the wrenching bend
cowers a persistent yearning,
a burning loneliness that drives
each fragile breath
we pass from lung to lung.

We roll alone down this road
of night that never ends,
tumble like a cage of seed and thorn,
from deep within our pain
a stout and solitary joy begins.

70

My Two Pocket Girl

After that dance at Copacabana
I begged her to give me two napkins
to write her phone number down twice
and slide one in each pocket for safe keeping.

My mother used to say how her dad, after losing his
    keys
or some important piece of paper, would always say:
*I didn't have this problem when I only had one pair of
    pants.*
Then she would tell the story

of when he was lucky enough
during the Great Depression
to work at the train station
and how his boss had asked him

to walk an expensive pedigreed dog
that was being shipped across country.
It was the prized pet of some rich, and I am sure, very
    important woman.
The dog got loose and ran away. My grandfather
    feared he'd be fired.

Then he caught a stray,
put it back in the crate labeled only "dog"
and put the crate back on the train.
I know the story was told for other reasons,

but sometimes I think about that stray.
Am I not like that dog?
Interrupted from life,
on a long ride to disappoint

some unknown, angry woman
further down the line.
This is the way it always happens.
I would not have this problem

if I only had one pair of pants.
Back to the girl at the dance, even with a napkin
in each pocket, I would still have lost her number
had she given it to me.

I go back to that same club
night after night after night
looking for that one dance, that one girl,
that one moment in her arms when I was more.

Sky Blues

A Bukka White concert at the Masonic Lodge on Delmar Street – a steamy St. Louis 90/90 night.

Stopped on the way to buy with a fake ID, a 99¢ bottle of iced MD 20-20 at the Delmar Street Liquor Store. Mogen David Wine – cool and juicy – like the stuff we used to drink on Passover with a little more sugar added for flavor and just enough formaldehyde to make you see things out of the corner of your eyes. No rabbis had blessed this shit. Carried it in the classic brown paper bag. No questions asked. We were as white as donut bags. We were the only two donut bags there that night to see Bukka White.

Bukka sang about salvation from the sweet girls up on Sugar Hill and about Jesus. A little too into it, cooling off with our Mad Dog wine, hooting our "Oh Yeahs" between those hesitations that make the blues breathe. No one minded the drunk young white boys, sitting on the floor, slapping out the cool concrete back beat only they could hear, a little creamy foam on a black sea of the blues. Bukka played it like it was. Laid it right down on our doorstep. Got to us where we lived.

Bukka called them "Sky Blues" because he reached up and "pulled them out of the sky." Milked his slide dobro with a butter knife. Squeezed out the blues until the power blacked out. Too many air conditioners in the suburbs sucking down too much juice. No iced MD 20-20 there to cool them down.

Bukka kept right on sliding down them blues, moaning rough as the Mississippi mud, pulling them out of the sky smooth as butter. With the mic dead, his voice rang out as pure as Passover wine. We were donut bags in the dark getting filled up with the blues.

Bukka was smiling as wide as the horizon when the lights came back on, his voice suddenly boomed through the Masonic Hall, echoing off the off-white walls.

I remember two donut bags stuffed and crumpled on the hard floor, as at home as litter.

Slow Blues in A What?
(or If a Harmonica Could Write a Poem)

to do what
to do what what
you want me
you want me
to do it
to do it to it
what what what

it is
it is
it is it
it is done here
there there
hear now
where is it
what it is
two to do
when we do it and
do to it what we do to it
here it is
here here here

now it is what
now now
what what what
to do what we do
from here to here
it is what it is
it is what we do
when we do it
if we do do it
before we blew it
before it's even due
I will do it to it too
to do what I do
from here to here

I will it to too
I will it to do it
all the way through it
to do what we do
too blue to undo
what the what what
done

Variations on William Carlos Williams

1.
I grasp you
like a wheel
hold you
as you turn
as imperfectly
sweet as a plum

how I cling
to your skin
shine in your tears
like a newborn
dripping with
the dew of birth

suddenly you
draw me
up through
the hoarse whispers
and dark sighs
of our humus

twirl me like a dream
fragile as stained glass
a coral cameo spinning
through the clouds
through the sun-bled air
into my new life

2.
this is to say
that what turns
your phrase
lifts me

that what you
saved for dessert
I am enjoying
for breakfast

that fruit ripens without apology
and the only thing
left in the icebox
is the cold

there never were
any chickens
nothing stays
white for long

Raven's Treat

Raven comes to my garden
in the cool green evening
head cocked and shiny,
feet wired to strawed earth.

He sips flat brown beer
from a muddy slug trap,
fishes out with scissor-sharp beak
the slugs that slid in last night.

A fine fellow always full of fancy,
he throws his dark head back,
letting the slugs slime down
his throat like raw oysters.

Raven tells me how tasty they are,
slowly marinated like this,
in barley malt
and warm sunshine,

and laughs how they are,
in fact, fat, juicy reincarnated
bar flies that couldn't
resist "just one more."

Crop-full, he dances boisterously,
a flickering shadow on golden straw,
cackling and crackling,
spitting out grim haiku,

cawing each one twice, each one twice:
   My obsidian
   eyes splash rivulets of black,
   dim the fragile dusk.

Never Too Old to Slam

I'm not too old to slam,
because I need
now more than ever
to spill this truth:
the older I am,
the more alive I feel.
I am a tattered
paradox of passion,
a dying ember
eager to explode
into flame.

The anger that has
raged inside me
for so long
holds up a giant,
final fuck-you finger
to the flaccid face of fate,
raises up its hissing head
and spits its cobra venom
into the great sucking
eye of death.

It's time for me to slam it
down. I'm finally old enough
to really say what I mean
and not give a shit what people think.
Look into the mirror of my words.
If you think I'm less than I am
because I'm older than I feel,
I'm talking to you. There is
nothing left but the truth.
I tell you this because
I'm done with blame.

Look at me,
and if you see yourself,
it's because we are the same.
I may finish before you start,
but we all run the same race.
For how long or at what pace
doesn't really matter.
It's the human race,
and we have no choice
but to run, and run we do,
and no one running
with their heart open
ever loses, and no one
reaching for more
leaves empty handed,
and not a single stride
goes to waste.

It's time to get down to it.
Our forever is now and
forever changing into then.
Nothing you can say
makes it easier to die.
The truth is simple:
we're lost without love.

As long as I'm alive,
I'll never forgive the greed
that rots our world,
that nips our heels
and turns our Eden
to wasteland.
Nor will I ever abide
the hate that
rips apart our souls,
if we don't take a stand.

We are a bursting
supernova of love,
silhouetted by
the lightning
of our desire.
When we smile,
we shine more brightly
than a billion stars.
When we grieve,
it is a hurricane of pain,
a deluge of hurt without end.

My brothers and sisters
are of all ages.
Together we are more
colorful than the fish
that glide among the coral,
more tenacious than wild thistle.
Together we wield the power
of the human heart,
there's nothing more potent,
nothing we cannot overcome.

I'm not too old or too white to slam,
because I'm half African,
half Asian, half Jew, half Arab,
half indigenous, half developed,
half wild, half dead, half human,
half animal, half budding green,
half dark night.
I am the dawning
half bright half-light.
My life is more
than half over,
but my half-life is infinite.
I've half a mind
to leave this half-assed
country if there was
somewhere else I could find
that was halfway decent.

No, I'm not too old, too white
or even too straight to slam,
because I'm half man,
half woman, half gay,
half lesbian, half trans,
half willing, half-witted and half-cocked.

I'm always halfway between
myself and somebody else
and always some when
between now and again.
I'm on my way to being me.

Being alive
is all about connection.
Nothing else matters.
There's nothing evil, nothing
wrong, nothing about you,
nothing inside of me,
nothing human I cannot love.

My brothers and sisters are misters
and misses, and men who love men,
and women who love women, and men
who were born women and women
who were born men, and men and women
who are both or neither a man or a woman.
It makes no difference.
How much I love you
has nothing to do with your color,
your gender, your dress,
who you fuck or how old
you aren't,
but with who you are.
It's all about the joy
of you becoming you.

I know now I'm not too old
to slam because I can still
see the beauty inside everyone.

I know no matter
what we think we want,
or how hard we try
to be someone else,
we can only ever be
who we truly are.

I'm not too old
to slam because
I'm not too old to love.

I sit on the ragged
edge of death's bed.
I blink and gulp the light,
like a goldfish gulps for air,
and decide each morning
to get up and live,
to love and become
and choose not to
sleep beyond the darkness.
If my heart is still beating,
I open it.

The longer I live,
the more I have
a need to give.
The more I give,
the more I have
to live for.

I'll never be
too old to care,
never too old to slam.

A Good Dog

It was white steam curling over the pot's lip,
the bumping cobs of corn bobbing in bubbles,
the thick, sun-warm, bleeding slices
of beefsteak tomatoes and, especially,
the yellow butter's languid pose

that signaled summer was finally here.
The previous November just days
after his twenty-third birthday, my brother was found
under a pile of decomposing leaves face
down in a deserted Missouri wood.

We heard it first on the St. Louis news:
After a month missing from a St. Charles's Radio Shack,
two employees found shot in back of head,
execution style, motive still not known
for the lunch time abduction.

For the first time that summer
Dad phoned Mom to "put the water on."
He was coming home with freshly picked sweet corn.
It was the only time I remember Mom forgot
to add her secret spoon of sugar to the pot.

We sat at the table closer than normal
around a small basket of wilting memories
gnawed by a nagging emptiness
not discussing that which
never made sense...

When Sister, our dog, snuck in to beg the summer food
she only just sniffed anyway, one stern look from Dad
and she sulked to her place by the kitchen door.
She laid down in trained disappointment,
persisting, almost human, a good dog.

Never Ask a Poet Directions
for Jared Smith

To start with
don't walk too fast.
It is best to lean
into each step
so as to feel the ground

move you.
Circle to your left
under the pitched arm
of the burning tree twisting
its flames toward the fired sky.

Don't forget to duck.
This way you may
enjoy the exquisite
pain of your passing
again and again.

It might go better yet
to model Alice
and make yourself
very, very small.
It may take most of your life

to cross the footprint
of the mother raccoon,
but do not look back
upon a path glittered with regret,
lest you fall like tears

from the eye
of your own making.
When you find that place
where her sharp claws
have punctured the dark loam,

stop and rest.
You may even need to sleep
before you go on.
Most do.
You will know

when you are ready:
the warm heave
of your breath
will wake you. Of course,
it is always dark.

When what little light there is
films the rounded stone like milky dew,
it will be time to move again.
Follow the ragged ravine
winding to your right

as if you were water.
Do not fixate
on the wiggle
of your falling.
Remember,

there is nowhere
to fall but down.
As you catch the hang of it,
you will begin to roar.
The clamor of everyone

you have ever known
will be echoing
vociferously inside you.
A few lusty
cries will rise

from this surge
only to resubmerge
just as they start
to make sense.
You will not be missed,

though it will seem
like forever
you are gone.
Eventually,
things settle down.

You become as flat
and smooth as
a velvet pool
in the moonlight.
There is nothing left

but yourself
as far as
you can see,
and still you
expand.

You will know
when you arrive
because it is like
you have never left.
Ask a poet

directions, only
when you realize
you have
no place
to go.

Time for Gertein Strewed
for Gertrude Stein

We know how little we know when we know
    how little time there is.
Time is there when we don't know.
Time is when we don't know how little time is.
Time is little when we know when time is.
Time is when we don't know when.
How little we know when we don't know.
How little time there is when we don't know.
How time is there we don't know.
We know a little about what we don't know.
We know there is a little to know about time.
Maybe time knows what we don't know.
We know we don't know what time knows.
We know we don't know how little there is to
    know.
We know we don't know how little there is.
We know we don't know how it is to be little.
We know there is little.
Time is when we know little.
Time doesn't know what we know.
Time doesn't know how little time is when we
    know.
Time doesn't know we are not time.

Circus of Mirrors

I paint my face with laughter and tears.
The clown I am to myself
thinks he runs the show,
lives in a circus of mirrors.

I pay for my tickets,
twisted strips as red as raw meat,
changing hands as smoothly
as the tools of a surgeon.

I come and go afraid,
not sure which side is real,
I lose myself
in mirror after mirror.

I live my reflection
over and over.
I dread the revenge of light
when it discovers the trap.

I watch the back and forth clown
prancing through a land he thinks he owns.
His face glistens and bloats
with the greed of the day.

He moves as musically as water,
as silently as light,
in a hurry to nowhere.
He does not believe I am real.

He wears the makeup of my pain,
frozen into a permanent smile.
His words tinkle as joyously
as breaking glass.

His face floats over the evening.
It follows me when I leave
like a lonely Mylar balloon
attached by an invisible string.

He aches in my dreams, steals the warmth from my sleep.
My cover is as thin as a sheet
of aluminum foil. I awake shivering and alone.
All is quiet.

The circus is a mere memory.
The mirrors in my house
are as still as they were
when no one was home.

There are strips of torn paper in my pockets
which could have been a poem.
I piece them together.
They slice to the bone.

They are like slivers of silvered glass,
shards of captured years,
each word a vicious side show,
a flood of living tears.

My hands bleed
all over them.
It is the story
of my life.

wings of haiku

lonely wasted heart

seek your ancient
home inside

uncover your joy

marble-fisted doubt

open the bright
shards of glass

diamonds in the light

The Visitors

walls of incandescent metal
the incessant whir of the electric
punctuated by busy clicks
of buttons and switches
my head inside the glass helmet
radiating splintered lines of color
like a feral plasma ball
jagged ridges of blue midnight
bolts of lavender, waves of deep forest green
the air was clean but tainted with the smell of ozone
and then in my mind everything at once flared clear
myriad petals of pastel light
fell around me like warm snow

I knew they meant well
I had followed the trail of broken rocket parts
to find them and then they invited me in
they were friendly enough
strangely familiar and gentle
their bodies were translucent
with lips tinged fuchsia
their breath smelled of amber laced with fennel
their gold-flecked eyes flickered as steadily
as the stars but warmer like points of flame
none of this matters I know
you just need to know I went in
of my own will and now I am fine

let me tell you though
what they told me
they said they
had come to bring us
what we all have always wanted
a gift wrapped in starlight
from the dark skies of their home
it all happened so quickly
a flash of current and the exquisite bliss
of being fully human
flooding through me
as if I had been as empty as a vase
and now you see I am blooming

Wonder Moment

My mantra is silence,
my eye, light,
my heart always
wells up with joy.

I breathe
iridescent wonder
into this moment
forever alive.

Bedside Manner
upon the passing of my mother

The dying have no sense
of when. Everything is
was, each breath,
a terrible wind.

The light of those they love
gathers like a tempestuous mob
shaking smoking torches
outside the window,

blazes like the rising sun,
flooding the river of glass
with the searing certainty
of inevitable dawn.

The dying always walk
the other way, forgetting
all paths lead back, like breathing,
the way in is the way out.

I was there when she tumbled
like a flaming magnolia
down the long well of herself.
I felt the exquisite weightlessness,
then her fear. What happens

at the bottom? She clenched
my hand in hers in mine in hers.
Although she was ashen as a tear of dust,
hollow as peeled snakeskin,

I asked if she remembered the time in temple
on Yon Kippur, when we both felt
the hand of her father's ghost
squeeze hers squeezing mine.

He came to tell you it's all right.
She remembers
to let go. Falls forever.
Nothing is more beautiful.

Walk in Beauty

Spring swims inside me.
As I step, the grass mumbles
something about the rain.

Grass feels no anger
as we waste our paradise.
Animals come

and go and always
green returns. Trees
do not hesitate

to burst bud.

Grief falls heavy
as I walk in beauty
through a breaking land.

Wind still
lifts
the great hawk,

as clouds laced red
with the smoke of sunset
fade to black.

Universal

Sunlit
seed heads nod
in eager waves.

Golden grass bends
in an agreeable wind
now and again:

same air
pulses through
each of us.

No matter
how old
or alone,

we bow our heads
to the same
light within.

Cruel Surgery

breath takes me in
to my root
my transcendence

to the wellspring
of the infinite
inside

where even
shadows crackle
with light

I embrace grief's
cruel surgery
and heal my heart

About the Author

M. D. Friedman is an award-winning poet, artist and musician who lives in Lafayette, Colorado. He often incorporates diverse musical elements such as blues harmonica and Native American flute improvisations into his spoken word performances. His *Visual Mantra* healing art collection is free to use at *FineArtMandalas.com*. His innovative, acoustic roots band, *Mad Dog Blues,* as well as his meditative free jazz ensemble, *Peddlers of Joy,* can be found playing live around Colorado. His website, *MDFriedman.com*, features links to all of M. D.'s creative pursuits.

Audio versions of the *Into Light* poems, performed by the poet, are available on all music streaming services, at audiobook outlets and on BandCamp.

Please see *LiquidLightPress.com/IntoLight.htm* for all things *Into Light* including links to live videos, e-books, digital poems and musical poems.

Acknowledgments

The author wishes to thank the editors of the following journals, presses, anthologies and organizations, where the poems listed below were first published, some in an earlier form.

Poems, previously appearing in magazines, e-zines and anthologies:
Turtle Island Quarterly (E-zine, 2013), "The Goddess Ate at Arby's"
Poetica Magazine (Fall 2013 Edition), "Bedside Manner"
IMPROV 2011 (Green Fuse Press anthology), "Rerun"
Poetry on Track, (Columbine Poets of Colorado anthology, 2013), "i wish now"
Inspired: Robin Dodge & the Masters of Art (Loveland Museum Ekphrastic Anthology, 2012), "Girl Braiding Hair"
Bent Ear Review (Muse Pie Press, 2013), "Never Too Old to Slam" (audio version)
Verse Wrights (E-zine, 2012), "The Last Time Dad Opened His Eyes," "Bedside Manner" and "Girl Braiding Hair"
Exception/ALL: Anthology of What It Means to Be Normal (Writing Heights Writers Association, 2023), "It's Easy to Be Normal"

Poems previously appearing as digital poem videos: "Never Ask a Poet Directions" (2012), "Know Where to Go Crazy" (2010) and "forever trespass" (2008)

Poems previously appearing as spoken word recordings or mixed into longer musical compositions:
Walking on the Sky (2013) album, the poem, "The Great Clock," was embedded into the tracks, "Crossing the Bridge" (Parts 1 & 2)
One World (2020) album, the poem, "Universal," was embedded into the track, "One Light"

Poems recorded with original music from the *Word* (2021) album:
"Two as One," "Know Where to Go Crazy," "Slow Blues in A What?" "Hooked ," "forever trespass," "The Long Drive Home from a Gig at 3 AM" and "Never Ask a Poet Directions"

Poems previously appearing in chapbooks:
The Body of the Mind (2000 – Lulu), "March 21, 1994," "The First Snow," "Highway 93 as KFML Goes Off the Air, 1975," "Time for Gertein Strewed," "The Door," "Circus of Mirrors," "The King of the United States," "The Last Time Dad Opened His Eyes," "Fetish for the Dark," "My Will" and "Simple Silence"

From Here to Here (2002 – Internet Poets' Cooperative), "As the Stars Go Out," "The Unwinding" and "Slow Blues in A What?"

Nothing Else Matters (2003 – Internet Poets' Cooperative), "Feasting in America", "A Good Dog," "Upon Turning Fifty," "Parting Shots," "A Pair of Apple Poems" and "The Super Bowl of the Muse"

Where We Reach (2005 – Lulu), "i wish now," "Variations on William Carlos Williams," "The Visitors," "My Two Pocket Girl," "Coupled Socks," "She Has a Mortgage on My Body and a Lien on My Soul," "Selling Ourselves" and "We Fly"

Leaning Toward Whole (2011 – Liquid Light Press), "The Return of Light," "The Great Clock," "Raven's Treat," "The Lost River," "Spring Love Poem," "Li Po Returns to His Lover in the Night," "Never Ask a Poet Directions," "Know Where to Go Crazy," "Bedside Manner" and "The Old Barn"

Some of the poems, sometimes in earlier versions, have been shared previously alone or as part of small collections in online posts to social networks or blogs or as performance audio or video recordings.

Other Books from Liquid Light Press

All books are available directly from *liquidlightpress.com*.

- *Leaning Toward Whole* by M. D. Friedman (2011) – Explores the poignant and personal. Also available as a groundbreaking multimedia enhanced e-book.
- *The Miracle Already Happening – Everyday Life with Rumi* by **Rosemerry Wahtola Trommer** (2011) – A special collection of poems full of heart, humor, peace and wisdom.
- *Spiral* by **Lynda La Rocca** (2012) – A compelling poetic and melodic discourse of the persistent cravings and fears inside of each of us.
- *From the Ashes* by **Wayne A. Gilbert** (2012) – A true masterpiece that gnaws at the heart with universal appeal.
- *ah* by **Rachel Kellum** (2012) – This poetry has a simplicity and clarity that cuts to the core of being human.
- *Catalyst* by **Jeremy Martin** (2012) – *Catalyst* may just launch you on a fiery ride into yourself.
- *Of Eyes and Iris* by **Erika Moss Gordon** (2013) – Beautiful yet poignant in its simplicity.
- *Your House Is Floating* by **Susan Whitmore** (2013) – As smooth, crisp and satisfying as olive oil on fresh garden greens.
- *Nowhere Near Morning* by **Jeffrey M. Bernstein** (2013) – An intimate embrace of what it means to be alive.
- *Harmonica* by **Cecele Allen Kraus** (2014) – *Harmonica* bristles with a shimmering music that heals the heart.
- *Surf Sounds* by **Roger Higgins** (2014) – Expertly crafted and superbly written, pulsing with the tides of the soul.
- *Black-Footed Country* by **Lindsay Wilson** (2015) – Like eating an artichoke, there are layers within thorny layers, each one more tender and subtle until you feast on the heart inside.
- *The Dice Throwers* by **Douglas Cole** (2015) – *The Dice Throwers* shines like a flashlight across the gritty dark alleys of the American soul, turning shattered glass into diamonds.
- *Lessons on Sleeping Alone* by **Megan E. Freeman** (2015) – While easily accessible, Megan's elegant writing is complexly layered with hard-won common sense and clarity.
- *The Offering* by **Eleanor Kedney** (2016) – A masterful, poetic tapestry woven from what makes us human.
- *This Town, Poems of Correspondence* by **Kyle Laws & Jared Smith** (2017) – This gifted collaboration on small town America between two of Colorado's finest poets will hit you where you live.
- *Pneuma* by **Jennifer Lothrigel** (2017) – *Pneuma* navigates the intuitive world of the self with both power and subtle grace.
- *Saved by the Dead* by **Robert Cooperman** (2018) – A poetic journey transcending nostalgia and exploring the residual impact of the 1960's counterculture in 21st century America.
- *Memory and Form* by **Nathan Ybanez** (2021) – A world bursting with beauty, pathos, vibrancy and connection.